The Write Way Book 1

PLOT Building

W. J. Manares

Ukiyoto Publishing

All global publishing rights are held by

Ukiyoto Publishing

Published in 2024

Content Copyright © W. J. Manares

ISBN 9789362692603

*All rights reserved.
No part of this publication may be reproduced,
transmitted, or stored in a retrieval system, in any
form by any means, electronic, mechanical,
photocopying, recording or otherwise, without the
prior permission of the publisher.*

The moral rights of the authors have been asserted.

*This book is sold subject to the condition that it shall
not by way of trade or otherwise, be lent, resold, hired
out or otherwise circulated, without the publisher's
prior consent, in any form of binding or cover other
than that in which it is published.*

www.ukiyoto.com

Written by a writer for other writers like you

Contents

Introduction	1
I. PLAN	3
A. Presentation	4
B. Listing	6
C. Acts	8
D. Next	10
II. LEARN	12
A. Lurk	13
B. Emulate	14
C. Ask	16
D. Research	18
E. Notes	21
III. OBSERVE	23
A. Obvious	24
B. Blurry	26
C. Sequence	29
D. Eloquence	31
E. Redundance	33

F. Views	35
G. Emotion	38
IV. TELL	41
A. Theme	42
B. Entertain	45
C. Lifelike	48
D. Lifetime	50
About the Author	52

Introduction
PLOT: A "Secret" Outline to Do Something.

Welcome to "The Write Way Book 1: Plot Building," a guide that unveils the clandestine art of storytelling and reveals why PLOT is the clandestine outline to craft compelling tales.

Plot, often shrouded in enigma and veiled in secrecy, is the silent architect that shapes the grand tapestries of literary creation. It is the clandestine whisper that guides characters through trials, triumphs, and transformation. Like a hidden map leading to unseen treasures, plot serves as the secret outline, the unspoken guide, to weaving magic with words.

Within the pages of this book, aspiring writers and seasoned wordsmiths alike will unravel the mysteries of plot building, learning how to harness its power to captivate readers, stir emotions, and leave a lasting imprint on the soul. Through intricate storytelling techniques, character development insights, and narrative structuring wisdom, discover why plot is not merely a roadmap but a hidden key to unlock the gates of unforgettable storytelling.

Join me on this literary journey as we delve into the heart of plot building, uncovering its secrets, unraveling its intricacies, and unleashing its

transformative magic upon the written page. Embrace the power of plot, and embark on an odyssey of creativity, inspiration, and storytelling mastery. Once again, welcome to "The Write Way Book 1: Plot Building," where the secret of plot awaits to be unveiled, and the enchantment of storytelling beckons you to write your own unforgettable tale.

- W. J. Manares, Author

June 8, 2024

I. PLAN

A. Presentation

1. Protagonist and Antagonist

When introducing the protagonist and antagonist in your story, it is important to establish their contrasting personalities, goals, and motives. The protagonist is the main character who drives the story forward, while the antagonist is the character who opposes or challenges the protagonist. Show their relationship and conflict through their interactions, actions, and dialogue.

2. From Start to Finish

Knowing your story from start to finish involves having a clear understanding of the character arcs, and thematic elements from beginning to end. This includes knowing the main events, twists, and resolution of the story. This comprehensive view allows you to effectively foreshadow, build tension, and create a cohesive narrative that keeps readers engaged.

3. Knowing the Ending Before Starting to Write

Understanding the ending of your book before starting to write it is crucial for maintaining focus and coherence in your storytelling. Knowing how your story concludes helps guide the development of characters, plot twists, and themes throughout the entire narrative. It also allows you to lay out clues and build up to a satisfying resolution that ties up loose ends and resonates with readers.

B. Listing

By organizing and making lists of these elements, you can ensure that your book's characters, settings, and events are well-developed, consistent, and engaging for your readers.

1. Names and Descriptions

- Create a list of all the main characters in your book, including their names and a brief description of who they are, their role in the story, and their personality traits.

- List out any important locations in your book, such as setting details, landmarks, and descriptions of the environment.

2. Background and Backstory

- Outline the background and backstory of each character, including their history, motivations, and any key events that have shaped who they are.

- Develop the backstory of important locations, including the history of the place, any significant events that have occurred there, and how it plays a role in the overall story.

3. Behavior and Physique

- Make a list of each character's behavior traits, such as how they interact with others, their flaws, strengths, and mannerisms.

- Describe the physical appearance of each character, including details such as height, weight, hair color, eye color, and any distinguishing features such as tattoos, etc.

4. Time and Events

- Create a timeline of events in your book, including the main plot points, key events, and any twists or turns that occur throughout the story.

- List out any important dates or time periods that play a significant role in the narrative, such as historical events, anniversaries, or key moments in the characters' lives.

C. Acts

1. Cause and Effect

Creating a plot based on cause and effect involves establishing a sequence of events where one action leads to another consequence, ultimately driving the story forward. To implement this in your plot, consider starting off with an inciting incident that sets everything in motion. This initial cause should lead to a series of events that provoke further actions and reactions from the characters, ultimately building towards a resolution or climax. Ensuring that each event has a clear cause and effect relationship will help maintain a sense of progression and coherence in your plot.

2. Problem and Solution

In constructing a plot around the problem and solution framework, it is essential to introduce a central conflict or obstacle that the protagonist must overcome. This problem serves as the driving force behind the narrative and motivates the characters to take action. As the story progresses, the protagonist may face various challenges and setbacks in their quest to solve the central problem. The resolution should come in the form of a solution or resolution that addresses the initial conflict, bringing closure to the story. This structure is particularly effective in creating tension and suspense, as readers are invested in seeing how the protagonist will overcome the obstacles they face.

3. Question and Answer

Using the question and answer format in building a plot involves posing a series of questions or mysteries that the characters must unravel throughout the story. These questions can range from personal dilemmas, to larger mysteries that drive the overall plot forward. As the characters seek answers and solutions to these questions, they may uncover new information or face unexpected challenges that push the story in new directions. The resolution of the plot should provide satisfying answers to the questions that have been posed, tying up loose ends and providing closure for the characters and the reader. This format can create a sense of intrigue and keep the reader engaged as they seek to uncover the answers along with the characters.

D. Next

1. Think of it as a Series even if it's a Standalone

Thinking of your book as a series, even if it's initially conceived as a standalone, can open up possibilities for future storytelling. By leaving certain plot threads unresolved or introducing new characters that can be further developed, you can create a rich universe that can be expanded upon in future books. This approach also allows you to build a loyal fan base who will eagerly anticipate the next installment.

2. Book 2 in Mind Before you Start Book 1

It's important to have a clear idea of where you want the story to go in the long term. This can involve outlining future plot points, character arcs, and themes that will be explored in later books. By laying this groundwork early on, you can ensure that there is a sense of continuity and cohesiveness. Additionally, it can be helpful to keep detailed notes on key events, character motivations, and unresolved plot threads that can be revisited in future installments. This will allow you to seamlessly transition from one book to the next, while also leaving room for surprises and unexpected developments along the way.

II. LEARN

A. Lurk

1. Lurk Like a Stalker

Lurking, in the context of writing, can indeed be a beneficial practice for plot building. By observing and spending time in one place, like a stalker of sorts, you can gain valuable insights and inspiration for your stories. This process allows you to immerse yourself in different environments, characters, and situations, leading to a deeper understanding of human behavior and the world around you.

Lurking helps you to capture the nuances of human interaction, emotions, and reactions, which are crucial elements in creating realistic and relatable characters. Paying attention to the details, you can develop a more authentic and vivid portrayal of characters' thoughts, feelings, and motivations.

Lurking also enables you to discover unique story ideas and plot twists. By immersing themselves in different settings or communities, you may stumble upon unexpected narratives, conflicts, or untold stories. These hidden gems can spark your imagination and become the foundation for compelling plotlines.

B. Emulate

1. Strive to Equal or Match other Writings and Authors

Emulating other writings and authors can be a valuable tool for writers to learn and improve their plot building skills. By striving to equal or match the works of established authors, you can gain insight into their techniques, narrative structures, and storytelling prowess.

When you emulate, you are essentially studying the work of others and dissecting what makes it successful. By closely examining the plots of renowned authors, you can identify patterns, pacing, and plot devices that engage readers and create a compelling narrative arc. This process allows you to learn from their expertise and apply similar techniques to your own writing.

Emulating also helps you understand the nuances of plot development. By analyzing how other authors build tension, create plot twists, and resolve conflicts, you can gain a deeper understanding of effective plot construction. Through this process, you can learn how to engage readers, maintain their interest, and deliver satisfying resolutions.

C. Ask

1. Anyone Ready to Give you a Random Answer Whether True or False

Asking random individuals for answers, whether true or false, can be an interesting approach to gather diverse perspectives and ideas for your plot building as a writer. This method can help you expand your creative thinking and consider alternative viewpoints that you may not have previously considered.

By soliciting random answers, you invite a range of ideas and possibilities that can spark your imagination. Sometimes, unexpected responses can challenge your existing notions and push you to think outside the box. This process encourages you to explore unconventional plot twists or character developments that might add depth and intrigue to your storytelling.

Moreover, engaging with different perspectives can help you better understand the varied experiences and viewpoints of your potential readers. It allows you to tap into the collective wisdom and diverse backgrounds of others, which can enrich your writing and make it more relatable to a wider audience.

However, it's important to approach this method with discernment and critical thinking. While random answers can be a valuable source of inspiration, it's crucial to evaluate and filter them based on your own storytelling goals and principles. Not every random answer may align with your vision or fit seamlessly into your plot. It's up to you as the writer to discern which ideas are worth incorporating and how they can enhance your narrative.

D. Research

Reading, watching, listening, and even hearing can all be valuable tools for writers' research. Each of these activities offers unique benefits, from exposing you to different writing styles and techniques to providing inspiration and insights into human experiences. By actively engaging in these activities, you can expand your creative horizons, enrich your plots, and develop a unique storytelling voice.

1. Read

Reading is an essential tool for any writer. It exposes you to different writing styles, genres, and narratives, which can inspire and inform your own plot building. By reading widely, you can gain insights into effective storytelling techniques, character development, world-building, and narrative structures. It also helps you expand your vocabulary and improve your overall writing skills. Reading news and other non-fiction materials can provide you with a wealth of knowledge and ideas that can be incorporated into your plots, making them more relevant and engaging.

2. Watch

Watching TV series, films/movies, and videos can be a valuable source of inspiration for writers. Visual storytelling can offer unique perspectives on plot development, character arcs, and creative storytelling techniques. By observing how scenes are structured, how characters are portrayed, and how conflicts are resolved, you can gain insights into effective plot building and pacing. Watching different genres and styles can broaden your understanding of storytelling possibilities, helping you think creatively and outside the box.

3. Listen

Listening, in the context of plot building, involves actively paying attention to the conversations and experiences of others. Engaging in meaningful conversations, participating in dialogue, and actively listening to people's stories can provide you with valuable insights and perspectives. By listening to diverse voices and experiences, you can develop more authentic and relatable characters, incorporate realistic dialogue, and explore various themes and conflicts. Truly listening to others can deepen your understanding of human emotions, motivations, and relationships, which can enhance the depth and complexity of your plots.

4. Hear

Hearing refers to the passive act of perceiving sounds without actively engaging or processing the information. While hearing alone may not significantly contribute to plot building, it can still serve as a source of inspiration. Everyday sounds, background noise, snippets of conversations, and even music can trigger ideas, spark emotions, and create a sensory atmosphere that can be incorporated into your writing. Paying attention to the sounds around you can evoke imagery and help you create vivid and immersive settings for your story.

E. Notes

1. Prepare to jot down anything, anywhere, everything, everywhere, whenever, wherever, whatever (etcetera)

Taking notes on the go can be a helpful way to remember important information, capture ideas, and stay organized. Here are some tips for jotting down notes on anything, anywhere, everything, everywhere, whenever, wherever, whatever, and so on:

a. Use a Portable Notebook or Journal

Keep a small notebook or journal with you at all times so you can jot down notes whenever inspiration strikes. You can also use a note-taking app on your phone or other electronic device.

b. Keep it Simple

Don't worry about writing complete sentences or perfect grammar. Just write down key words or phrases that will help you remember the main points later on.

c. Use Shorthand

Develop your own shorthand system to quickly jot down notes without having to write out every word. This can help you capture information more efficiently.

d. Organize your Notes

Use headings, bullets, and numbering to organize your notes and make them easier to review later on. You can also use different colors or symbols to help distinguish between different types of information.

e. Capture Visuals

If you're in a hurry or don't have time to write down a lot of information, consider taking a quick photo or sketch to capture visual details that you can refer back to later.

f. Review and Revise

Take time to review your notes regularly and make any necessary revisions or additions. This will help reinforce the information in your memory and ensure that your notes are accurate and up to date.

III. OBSERVE

A. Obvious

1. Facts (could change)

Pay attention to the facts presented in your plot. These could include details such as character actions, dialogue, and setting descriptions. Consider how these facts contribute to the overall story and whether they are consistent throughout.

2. Truth (constant)

Focus on revealing the truth in your plot. This could be the underlying theme or message you want to convey, or the ultimate outcome of the story. The truth should remain constant and clear as the plot unfolds.

3. Trivial

Don't get caught up in trivial details that do not significantly impact the plot. While small details can add depth to your story, make sure they serve a purpose in moving the plot forward.

4. General Knowledge

Consider incorporating general knowledge or

common themes in your plot. This can help ground the story in a familiar context for readers and make it easier for them to follow along. However, be sure to add your own unique twists and perspectives to keep the plot engaging and original.

B. Blurry

1. Cultural Gap

Conduct a research on the cultures you are writing about. This could involve reading books, watching documentaries, or speaking with individuals from that culture to gain a deeper understanding of their beliefs, values, and traditions. Once you have a better understanding of the culture, you can adjust your plot accordingly to ensure that it is accurately represented.

2. Worldview

Worldview refers to the overall perspective or outlook of a character or group of characters in a story. It can be helpful to consider the motivations, beliefs, and experiences that shape your characters' perspectives. This can help you understand why characters make certain decisions or react in certain ways throughout the plot.

3. Mindset

It can be helpful to think about the mental and emotional state of your characters at different points in the story. You can clarify any uncertainties by digging deeper into their thoughts, feelings, and motivations to ensure that their actions are consistent and believable.

4. Unclear

If certain parts of your plot are unclear, it may be helpful to step back and reevaluate the overall structure and pacing of your story. Consider whether there are any gaps in information or inconsistencies in the plot that need to be addressed.

5. Gray Areas

Gray areas in plot building can add complexity and depth to a story, but they can also be confusing for readers if not handled carefully. It can be helpful to provide more context or background information to help readers understand the nuances of the situation. You can also consider adding additional scenes or dialogue to flesh out these gray areas and provide more clarity for the reader.

6. Tricky

Some parts of plot building can be tricky to navigate, especially when dealing with complex themes or conflicting motivations. It can be helpful to seek feedback from beta readers or writing peers who can offer fresh perspectives and insights. You can also consider revisiting these sections multiple times during the editing process to ensure that they are clear and cohesive within the larger narrative.

7. Confusing

If certain aspects of your plot are confusing, it may be helpful to revisit and revise these sections to provide more clarity and coherence. This could involve simplifying complex plot points, adding additional context or explanation, or restructuring the narrative to ensure that the story flows logically and effectively. Ultimately, the goal is to create a plot that is engaging and easy for readers to follow.

C. Sequence

As a writer, observing the sequence in plot building is crucial for creating a compelling story. Here are four approaches you can consider:

1. Step by Step

This approach involves developing your plot in a linear fashion, starting from the beginning and progressing to the end. You carefully craft each event, building upon the previous one. This method allows for a clear and logical progression of the story.

2. Procedures

Think of this approach as creating a set of guidelines or procedures for yourself as a writer. You establish certain rules or principles to follow while constructing your plot. These procedures can include elements such as introducing the conflict, escalating tension, and resolving the story's main conflict.

3. Road Map

Visualize your plot as a road map, with key events acting as milestones along the way. Plan out these major plot points in advance, ensuring that they are strategically placed to maintain the reader's interest. This approach allows for flexibility in filling in the details between these significant moments.

4. Timeline

Creating a timeline can be helpful in plotting your story's sequence. Map out the events and actions of your characters in chronological order, ensuring that there is a logical progression of events. This approach allows you to visualize the overall structure of your story and identify any gaps or inconsistencies.

D. Eloquence

Eloquence in plot building is achieved through a combination of clear and coherent storytelling, smooth transitions, and evocative language. Strive to create a narrative that flows seamlessly, engaging your readers and leaving them enthralled by the story you're weaving.

1. Clarity of Events

To maintain eloquence in your plot, it's important to ensure that the events are clear and easily understandable. Avoid convoluted or confusing plotlines that might confuse your readers. Clearly establish the cause-and-effect relationships between events, allowing for a smooth flow of the story. This clarity will help your readers follow along and stay engaged with the plot.

2. Smooth

Eloquence in plot building also involves delivering the story in a smooth and seamless manner. Transition between scenes and events in a way that feels natural, avoiding abrupt shifts that may disrupt the reader's immersion. Use appropriate pacing to maintain a balanced rhythm, ensuring that the plot unfolds at a pace that keeps the reader invested without feeling rushed or dragged out.

Additionally, pay attention to the language and writing style you employ. Choose words and phrases that enhance the elegance of your prose, creating a rich and immersive reading experience. Use descriptive and evocative language when necessary, but also be mindful of maintaining a balance so as not to overshadow the plot itself.

E. Redundance

Avoiding redundancy in plot building is crucial for keeping your story fresh, engaging, and captivating. Here are three strategies to help you achieve this:

1. Repetitive Narrative

Repetition can quickly become monotonous and bore your readers. To avoid this, strive for variety in your storytelling. Vary the pacing, tone, and structure of your narrative. Introduce new elements, conflicts, or twists to keep the plot dynamic and unpredictable. By avoiding repetitive patterns, you'll maintain the reader's interest and prevent the story from becoming stagnant.

2. Take it or Leave it

Sometimes, as a writer, you may feel attached to certain plot points, scenes, or characters that don't contribute significantly to the overall story. In such cases, it's important to assess whether these elements truly enhance the plot or if they can be removed without affecting the narrative's coherence. Be willing to let go of unnecessary or redundant aspects. This will streamline your plot, allowing the essential elements to shine and making the story more focused and impactful.

3. Originality Ain't Always Cool

While originality is desirable in storytelling, it's important to strike a balance. Being too focused on being completely unique can lead to forced or contrived plot elements. Remember that there are universal themes and archetypal story structures that resonate with readers. Embrace these elements and add your unique twist to them. Don't be afraid to draw inspiration from existing works or established storytelling techniques. By blending the familiar with your own creative ideas, you can create a plot that feels fresh and compelling while still being relatable to your audience.

F. Views

By carefully considering the point of view, narration, introduction, and outro or conclusion in your plot building, you can effectively incorporate diverse views. This will enrich your storytelling, create engaging conflicts, and offer readers a multi-dimensional experience that encourages critical thinking and reflection.

1. Point of View (POV)

The choice of POV determines whose perspective the story is told from. It greatly influences how readers experience the plot. Decide whether you want to use first-person (narrator as a character), third-person limited (narrator focuses on one character's thoughts and feelings), or third-person omniscient (narrator knows all characters' thoughts and feelings) POV. Each has its advantages and limitations, so choose the one that best serves your story and helps convey the desired views effectively.

2. Narration and Narrator

The way your story is narrated can significantly impact the readers' understanding and connection to the plot. Consider the tone, voice, and reliability of your narrator. They can provide a particular viewpoint or bias, shaping the readers' perception of events. Explore different narrative techniques like stream of consciousness, unreliable narration, or multiple narrators to offer diverse perspectives and add depth to your plot.

3. Intro

The beginning of your story sets the stage for the plot and introduces the main characters. Take advantage of this opportunity to present different views. Introduce characters with varying backgrounds, beliefs, or motivations. This diversity will create conflicts and tensions that drive the plot forward. By establishing contrasting viewpoints early on, you can engage readers and provide them with multiple perspectives to consider.

4. Outro or Conclusion

The ending of your story is where you can resolve conflicts and wrap up the plot. Consider how you want to address the different views presented throughout the narrative. You can opt for a conclusive ending that favors one viewpoint, or you can leave some questions unanswered, allowing readers to draw their own conclusions. The way you conclude the plot can leave a lasting impact on readers and shape their overall perception of the story.

G. Emotion

By being sensitive, filling and feeling, and engaging yourself emotionally, you can effectively observe and portray emotions in your plot building. This will bring your characters to life, create a deeper connection with your readers, and make your story resonate on a profound emotional level. Observing and incorporating emotions into plot building is crucial for creating engaging and impactful stories. Here are three strategies for writers to effectively observe emotions:

1. Be Sensitive

As a writer, it's important to be sensitive to the emotions of your characters and the situations they find themselves in. Pay close attention to the nuances of human emotions, both subtle and intense. Observe how people express their emotions through body language, facial expressions, and dialogue. Take note of how different emotions are triggered and how they evolve and change over time. By being sensitive to the emotional experiences of others, you can develop well-rounded and relatable characters that resonate with your readers.

2. Fill and Feel

To effectively portray emotions in your writing, you need to immerse yourself in the emotional experiences of your characters. Put yourself in their shoes and imagine how they would feel in various situations. Consider their backgrounds, motivations, and personal histories to understand how these factors shape their emotional responses. Take the time to fully explore and understand the range of emotions your characters may experience, from joy and love to fear and anger. By filling yourself with these emotions, you'll be better equipped to convey them authentically on the page.

3. Engage Yourself

Engaging yourself emotionally in your writing is essential for creating a genuine connection between your readers and your story. Allow yourself to feel the emotions you want to convey as you write. If you're writing a scene that should evoke sadness, tap into your own feelings of sadness. If you're writing a joyous moment, let yourself experience the joy. By engaging your own emotions, you can infuse your writing with authenticity and depth. Remember to also take care of yourself emotionally during this process, as delving into intense emotions can be draining.

IV. TELL

A. Theme

1. Stick to It

Telling about the theme in plot building is crucial for writers as it provides a central focus and underlying message to their story. Here are some strategies for effectively conveying the theme and the reasons why sticking to it is important:

a. Identify the Theme

Before you can effectively tell about the theme, it's important to identify it first. Reflect on the core message or idea you want to convey through your story. What universal truths, values, or concepts do you want to explore? Once you have clarity on the theme, you can then begin shaping your plot around it.

b. Show, Don't Tell

Instead of directly stating the theme, it is often more effective to show it through the actions, choices, and conflicts of your characters. Develop situations and dilemmas that allow the theme to naturally emerge. Allow your readers to discover the theme for themselves through the experiences and growth of the characters. This approach creates a more engaging and thought-provoking reading experience.

c. Consistency and Coherence

Sticking to the theme throughout your plot is crucial for maintaining consistency and coherence in your story. The theme acts as a guiding force, ensuring that every aspect of your plot, from character development to the resolution of conflicts, aligns with and reinforces the central message you want to convey. By staying true to the theme, you create a cohesive narrative that resonates with readers and leaves a lasting impact.

d. Depth and Complexity

A well-developed theme adds depth and complexity to your story. It allows you to explore different perspectives, moral dilemmas, and societal issues. By delving into the nuances and complexities of the theme, you create a richer and more layered narrative that engages readers on multiple levels. This depth not only enhances the storytelling experience but also invites readers to reflect and contemplate the themes long after they have finished reading.

e. Emotional Connection:

Sticking to the theme helps create a stronger emotional connection between the readers and your story. When the theme is clearly conveyed and explored throughout the plot, it resonates with readers' own experiences, beliefs, and values. This emotional resonance allows readers to connect with the characters and the story on a deeper level, fostering a sense of empathy and investment in the outcome.

In summary, telling about the theme in plot building is essential for writers as it provides a central focus and underlying message to their story. By identifying the theme, showing it through character actions, maintaining consistency, exploring depth and complexity, and creating emotional connections, writers can effectively convey their themes and create impactful and meaningful narratives. Sticking to the theme ensures that your story remains focused and purposeful, resulting in a more compelling and memorable reading experience.

B. Entertain

Telling an entertaining narrative in plot building is essential for engaging readers and keeping them hooked throughout your story. Here are some strategies to effectively accomplish this, with a focus on grabbing attention and hooking readers, and incorporating human-interest topics:

1. Grab Attention and Hook the Reader into your Story

To grab attention from the start, consider using an intriguing opening line, an unexpected event, or an intriguing question. By starting with something that piques readers' curiosity or creates a sense of intrigue, you can immediately grab their attention and compel them to continue reading.

Once you've grabbed attention, it's important to hook readers and keep them invested in your story. This can be achieved through various techniques such as creating relatable and likable characters, building suspense and tension through conflicts and challenges, and introducing plot twists and surprises. Engaging dialogue, vivid descriptions, and well-paced action can also help maintain readers' interest and keep them turning the pages.

To make your narrative more engaging, appeal to the senses by incorporating vivid descriptions and sensory details. By painting a visual and sensory landscape, you can transport readers into your story and make them feel immersed in the world you've created.

2. Human-Interest Topics

Human-interest topics are those that resonate with readers on an emotional level. They often involve universal experiences, emotions, or moral dilemmas that readers can relate to. By incorporating these topics into your plot, you can create a deeper connection with your readers. Explore themes such as love, loss, friendship, family dynamics, personal growth, or overcoming adversity. By tapping into these human experiences, you can evoke empathy, create emotional investment, and make your story more compelling and relatable.

Humor is an effective tool to entertain readers and add an element of lightness to your narrative. Incorporate witty dialogue, clever wordplay, or humorous situations to provide moments of levity and keep readers engaged. However, it's important to ensure the humor aligns with the tone and genre of your story, and doesn't detract from the overall plot or themes.

Intrigue and mystery can be powerful elements in storytelling. By introducing unresolved questions, hidden motives, or enigmatic characters, you can create a sense of curiosity and keep readers guessing. As the plot unfolds, gradually reveal clues and information, building anticipation and compelling readers to uncover the truth.

C. Lifelike

By incorporating these elements into your writing process, you can craft a narrative that feels lifelike and immersive, drawing readers in and keeping them engaged from beginning to end.

1. Full of Emotions

Infuse your storytelling with a range of emotions to make your characters and their experiences feel more authentic and relatable.

2. Make It Alive

Use vivid descriptions and engaging details to bring your scenes to life, enabling readers to visualize the settings and actions within your narrative.

3. Relatable

Create characters that readers can relate to by giving them depth, flaws, strengths, and believable motivations. This connection will draw readers into the story more effectively.

4. Reality Turned to Fiction

Ground your narrative in realistic elements, even if the overall story veers into the realms of fantasy or science fiction. This juxtaposition can make the story feel more tangible and engaging.

5. Not Only Verbal but "Verb All"

Don't just rely on dialogue to move the story forward. Use active verbs to describe actions and events in a way that keeps the narrative dynamic and engaging.

6. Act as You Write

By embodying the emotions and experiences of your characters, you can more effectively convey them to your readers.

D. Lifetime

Telling stories that stand the test of time and remain in the hearts and minds of readers for a lifetime is a lofty goal for any writer. Here are some strategies to help create lasting stories in plot building:

1. Legendary

Strive to create a piece of writing that reflects your unique voice, perspective, and creativity. Infuse your work with passion and authenticity, creating a story that is unmistakably yours. Make bold choices, take risks, and don't be afraid to experiment with unconventional storytelling techniques.

2. The Best of Time

Focus on creating a story that resonates deeply with readers on a personal level, rather than solely aiming for commercial success. While bestsellers may see temporary popularity, enduring stories are those that evoke strong emotions, provoke thought, and leave a lasting impact on the reader.

3. Lingering

Aim to craft a narrative that lingers in the minds of your audience long after they have finished reading. Create complex characters, richly detailed settings, and thought-provoking themes that stay with readers, sparking discussions and reflections even after the final page is turned.

By combining your unique voice and vision with powerful storytelling techniques, you can create stories that transcend time and leave a lasting legacy in the literary world. Focus on authenticity, emotional depth, and meaningful storytelling to craft narratives that will be cherished and remembered for generations to come.

Copyright © 2024 by W. J. Manares. All rights reserved.

About the Author

W. J. Manares

The Sardonic yet Whimsical Author of the Philippines W. J. Manares a. k. a. Willer Jun Araneta Manares is a one-of-a-kind persona in the literary scene of Aklan - the oldest province in the Philippines. He came out from his mother's birth canal on the 1st day of June, year 1985.

He came from a prominent Hispanic family. A legitimate member of Familia Araneta (Araneta Family) in the Philippines, included in its 7th generation, to be exact.

He's the Philippine Brand Ambassador of Noel Lorenz House of Fiction (NLHF - India), a common member of The Aklan Literati (AkLit), and one the common poets of Common Literature Period, a movement founded by Sourav Sarkar. He is a member of The Church of the Flying Spaghetti Monster and Philippine Pastafarian Church.

He loves everything erotic and sci-fi. A volunteer teacher with a philanthropic heart. And a freelance musical coach if needed. A lesser-known writer and worldbuilder who was influenced by the Superstar, Piers Anthony. He built the worlds of Stripes Archipelago, Nation of Tseicurdia and Land of Toto. His poems can be read in the anthologies edited by Sourav Sarkar. He's a Charles Bukowski and Spike Milligan admirer.

Seventeen of his books are published by Ukiyoto Publishing. And his more than 20 other books are published by other publishers.

Sometimes, he's a songwriter and loves to strum the guitar and sing. He loves the music of Rammstein, Red Hot Chili Peppers, Green Day, Eagle-Eye Cherry and Toad the Wet Sprocket.

When not writing, he's in his own library, reading and stacking his collection of books up on the shelves again and again. He loves the taste of cinnamon sometimes. He enjoys living his peculiar life near the gateway to the paradise island of Boracay.

www.ingramcontent.com/pod-product-compliance
Lightning Source LLC
LaVergne TN
LVHW041552070526
838199LV00046B/1916